Contents

What are Rainforests?

Imagine yourself in a dense, green forest. It's midday, but here on the ground there's lots of shade, provided by the huge trees that tower 60 metres or more above you. Every now and then, you stumble on an exposed root. The sweat is soaking through your shirt in the hot, damp atmosphere as your boots tramp through a carpet of leaves that cover the muddy ground. The air around you is filled with sounds – the buzzing of insects and the strange calls of birds and monkeys. Occasionally a grunt from the undergrowth startles you as you walk through the rainforest.

Tropical rainforests

Most rainforests are situated in the tropics – the warmest part of the Earth, which lies between the tropics of Cancer and Capricorn, 23.5 degrees north and south of the Equator. Tropical rainforests cover around 6 per cent of the planet's surface. Once, before we started clearing them, they covered up to 14 per cent. They experience annual rainfall of at least 2.5 metres, with some receiving up to 10 metres of rain each year.

Temperatures rarely fall below 20°C and can exceed 30°C. Humidity in the rainforest can reach up to 100 per cent. As the sun is almost directly overhead throughout the year, there are no distinct seasons. Altogether, tropical rainforests still cover about 15 million square kilometres of the planet's land surface. Key rainforest zones are the Amazon rainforest in Central and South America (45 per cent), the Congo

FACTS and FIGURES

RAINFOREST STATISTICS

- Every second, a slice of rainforest the size of a football field is mowed down. That's 86,400 football fields of rainforest per day, or over 31 million football fields of rainforest each year.

- Covering less than 2 per cent of the Earth's total surface area, the world's rainforests are home to 50 per cent of the Earth's plants and animals.

Source: The Nature Conservancy, www.nature.org

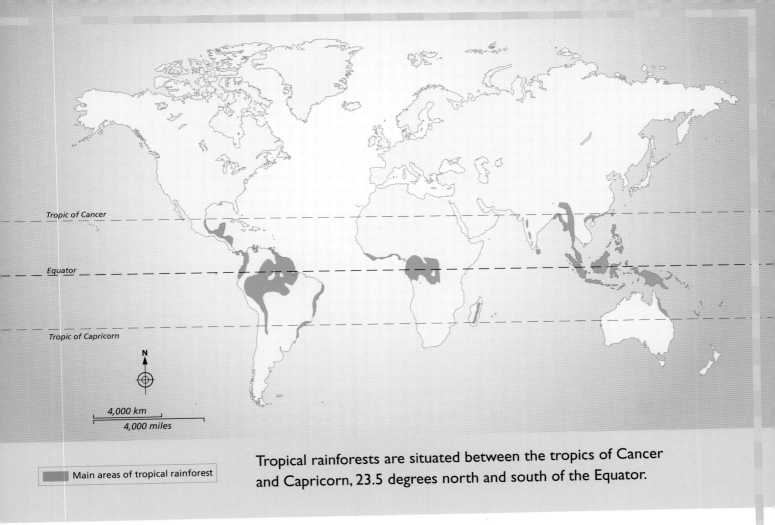

Tropical rainforests are situated between the tropics of Cancer and Capricorn, 23.5 degrees north and south of the Equator.

Main areas of tropical rainforest

Basin of Central Africa (30 per cent), South-East Asia (16 per cent) and Australasia (9 per cent).

Temperate rainforests

Temperate rainforests are situated in the Earth's temperate zones – between the Tropic of Cancer and the Arctic Zone in the northern hemisphere, and between the Tropic of Capricorn and the Antarctic Zone in the southern hemisphere. They are much rarer than tropical rainforests and are mostly located near the sea. Examples can be found in western North America, Japan, Chile, Argentina, Taiwan, Australia, New Zealand and some parts of East Asia.

Rainforests are among the oldest and richest habitats on the planet. They are home to more than half of all the Earth's living species, but they are also some of the planet's most threatened environments. This book will focus on the issues facing *tropical* rainforests.

What lives there?

Rainforests are home to an enormous variety of species. In total, perhaps

40 million different animal and plant species live there. In just 6.4 square kilometres of tropical rainforest, you might find 750 species of tree, 1,500 different kinds of flowering plants, 400 bird species, 150 types of butterfly, 125 different mammals and 60 varieties of amphibians!

Many of the plants that grow in the rainforest may have uses as medicines. Less than 1 per cent of tropical plants have been tested so far for medicinal purposes; even so, one in four ingredients in all our Western medicines can be traced back to the rainforest. For example, the rosy periwinkle, which is found in the rainforests of Madagascar, is effective in the treatment of leukaemia.

Yet despite this amazing array of potentially useful medicines and the enormous biodiversity (range and variety of species to be found within a given habitat) of the rainforests, huge amounts of the rainforest are being destroyed each year. About 150,000 square kilometres of tropical rainforest are cut down and burned every year and this destruction releases more carbon dioxide (a gas that is linked to climate change – see page 11) into the atmosphere than all the cars, trucks, buses and planes on the planet put together!

Who lives there?

Up to 500 million people depend on the tropical rainforest for their homes, food and livelihoods. Among these are the

PERSPECTIVES

RESPECTING THE LAND

Our land has to be respected. Our land is our heritage, a heritage which protects us.

Davi Kopenwa, leading spokesman for the Yanomami Indians of the Brazilian Amazon.

60 million or so indigenous people – the tribes who have lived in the forests for centuries, following a traditional way of life. These tribes, including the Kayapo and Yanomami of the Amazon, have passed on through the generations a deep knowledge of medicinal plants, of hunting and of how to grow and collect food from the forests without causing permanent damage. This has allowed them to coexist in harmony with the other creatures and plants of the rainforest.

Today, increasing numbers of settlers are moving into the rainforests – people with no interest in living in harmony with the forest. Some are poor farmers who move into the rainforest because no one owns the land they want to settle. They clear the trees so they can grow crops to feed themselves and their families. Far more damagingly,

A Baka tribesman from Cameroon snares a duiker. Rainforest peoples never take more than they need from the forest.

rainforests are also being cleared on an industrial scale to make way for huge farms, mines, logging operations and even hydroelectric power schemes (see p21).

Rainforest products

Many of the goods we get from rainforests are only obtained by causing damage or destruction. For example, many rainforest trees are felled for timber – an industry worth US$16 billion a year. Also, palm oil is grown in plantations that have been created by destroying the rainforests in Indonesia and Malaysia. Palm oil is used in about one in ten of the items you buy at the supermarket, including biscuits, cakes and even lipstick and floor polish!

Cattle ranching is another destroyer of the rainforest. Brazil, which contains most of the Amazon rainforest, is now the world's biggest exporter of beef. In fact, Brazil has more cows than people – and it has a human population of over 185 million!

Planetary climate control

Rainforests regulate temperature and weather far beyond the forests themselves. They help bring about regular rainfall, preventing both floods and droughts. Every day, vast amounts of water evaporate from the forest floor and from the leaves of the trees in the tropical heat. The water vapour rises and condenses into clouds high above the forest, then falls as rain later in the afternoon as the temperature decreases.

The daily cycle of evaporation and rainfall means that the forest gets neither too dry, nor wet enough to cause flooding. The clouds that form over the rainforests often travel far beyond the forests, giving many countries the fresh water they need for drinking and for growing crops.

Importantly for the planet, rainforests also sequester (lock away) huge amounts of carbon. The trees and plants take carbon dioxide from the air, and water from the ground, which they combine with sunlight to create the simple sugars they need to live and grow. This process is called photosynthesis. As a by-product of photosynthesis, the rainforests create

PERSPECTIVES

THE THREAT OF DEFORESTATION

If we lose the battle against tropical deforestation, we lose the battle against climate change.

HRH Prince Charles

The greatest danger hanging over our children and grandchildren is initiation of changes that will be irreversible on any time scale that humans can imagine.

James Hansen, head of NASA Goddard Institute for Space Studies

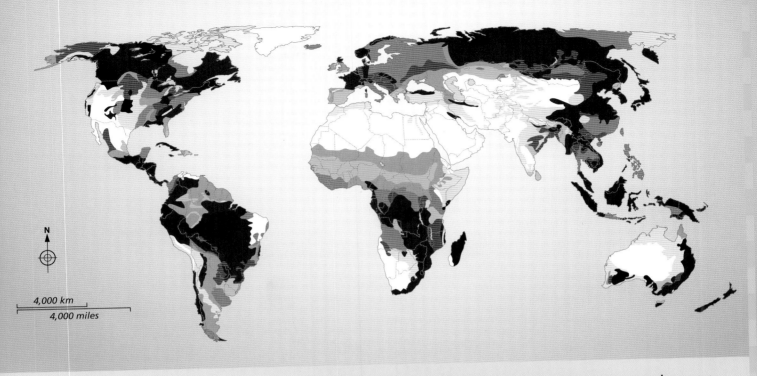

4,000 km

4,000 miles

This map clearly shows how rainforests are among the most heavily exploited forests on the planet. Only the forests of North America and South Australia are being depleted more quickly.

oxygen, which we need to breathe. The plants of the rainforest sequester far more carbon per hectare than plants living in any other land-based habitat – woodland, meadow or heathland for example.

When the rainforests are cleared, they are normally burned, which means that all of the carbon they were storing is released back into the atmosphere as carbon dioxide. Carbon dioxide occurs naturally in the atmosphere and helps to trap the sun's heat when it is reflected off the planet's surface. This is called the greenhouse effect because it is similar to the way glass traps

heat in a greenhouse. For this reason, carbon dioxide is known as a 'greenhouse gas'. The more carbon dioxide there is in the atmosphere, the more heat is trapped, and the warmer the planet becomes – at least in some places. So the destruction of the rainforests is a major contributor to global climate change.

The rest of this book will look at the issues that threaten rainforests across the globe. We will focus on particular regions to give examples of each of the issues – but many, if not all, the issues are common to tropical rainforests everywhere.

2: Farming in the Amazon Rainforest

The Amazon rainforest in South America makes up 45 per cent of the world's remaining tropical rainforest, covering almost 5.2 million square kilometres. It spreads across Brazil, Bolivia, Peru, Colombia, Ecuador, Venezuela, Guyana, Suriname and French Guiana. Brazil is the richest and most densely populated of the countries covered by the Amazon; it also has the highest rate of deforestation.

Since 1970, around 600,000 square kilometres of the Amazon rainforest have been lost. Between 2000 and 2006 alone, nearly 150,000 square kilometres of the forest were destroyed – that's an area bigger than the whole of Greece! Why has Brazil lost so much rainforest in such a short time?

Shifting cultivation

About one-third of the more recent loss of forest is due to 'shifting cultivators'. These are poor farmers who move into the forest to grow crops. Often, they have moved there after being forced off their land by big corporations looking to set up large-scale operations in areas of the forest – perhaps a new cattle ranch, soya plantation or a mine. In Brazil, many poor people are given areas of forest to cultivate by the government in a bid to make them self-sufficient.

Shifting cultivators clear patches of rainforest for themselves, mostly by cutting down the trees and burning them – a process known as 'slash and burn'. Many of them use the roads that have been carved through the forest by logging or mining

CASE STUDY

KAYAPO CULTIVATORS

Shifting cultivation, as practised by indigenous peoples, used to be sustainable. The Kayapo Indians of Brazil clear an area by cutting down trees and setting a fire. They build houses from the wood and foliage. Further trees are cut down to extend the clearing and feed their fires. The ash provides nutrients for the soil. Women plant manioc, yams, beans and pumpkins. After four or five harvests, they move on. In the past, they would not have returned to that land until it had recovered its fertility (about 50 years later). Now, pressures from plantations and ranches mean that they often have to return much sooner, before the rainforest soil has recovered.

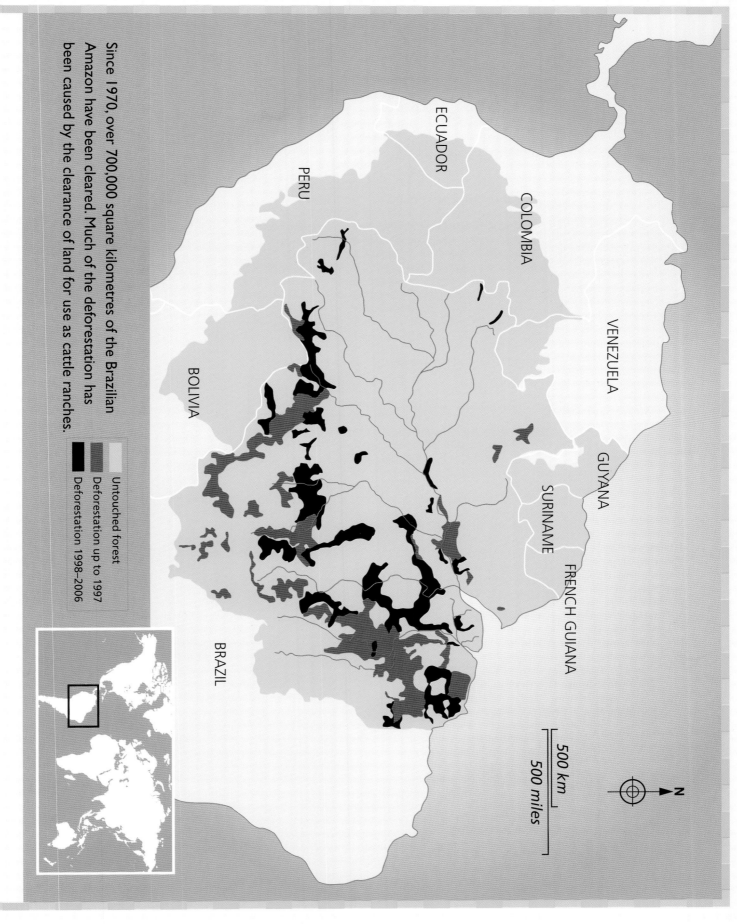

Since 1970, over 700,000 square kilometres of the Brazilian Amazon have been cleared. Much of the deforestation has been caused by the clearance of land for use as cattle ranches.

Untouched forest
Deforestation up to 1997
Deforestation 1998–2006

ECUADOR

PERU

COLOMBIA

VENEZUELA

GUYANA

SURINAME

FRENCH GUIANA

BOLIVIA

BRAZIL

500 km
500 miles

N

companies to gain access to areas of land deep in the forest. They use the land they clear to grow crops like bananas, palms, rice, maize or manioc.

Rainforest soil is very thin and lacking in nutrients. The reason that the forests appear so fertile is that dead leaves and animals are constantly being recycled. As the dead matter rots into the forest floor, it enriches the soil, allowing the forest to grow. When the trees are cleared to make way for crops, the supply of nutrients disappears with them. As a result, after a couple of years, the soil becomes less fertile, so the farmers clear new areas.

Individually these farmers do not use up much land – each one clears at least one hectare per year – but with an estimated 500,000 of them at work in the Brazilian Amazon, the impact of their activities soon adds up! Tens of thousands of small forest fires are observable by satellite every year.

The forests make way for cows

The bulk of the farming-related deforestation is not, however, caused by shifting cultivators. According to estimates by Greenpeace, up to 80 per cent of the destruction is caused by a few wealthy farmers, who create enormous ranches for their cattle to graze on.

How can the cattle herders afford to keep turning more and more rainforest land into pasture for their herds? They can do this quite easily, as much of the forest is not owned by anybody and, according to Brazilian law, if someone clears some forest, puts a few cattle on the land and leaves them there for a year, they are deemed to 'own' the land.

The destruction of the rainforest to create pasture for cattle causes problems. Whilst one hectare of cleared land may be productive enough to support one cow for a year or two after the forest is cleared, the

thin, poor rainforest soil is quickly eroded without tree roots to hold it together. After about seven years, that same cow may need to graze five or six hectares to survive for a year.

What's the beef with beef?

Solutions to the problems caused by cattle ranching are still a long way off. Brazil has global dominance in the beef

FACTS and FIGURES

CATTLE RANCHING

Cattle ranching is now the biggest cause of deforestation in the Amazon. Nearly 80 per cent of deforested areas in Brazil are used for pasture.

Greenpeace, January 2009

The blackened trunks of trees are sad reminders that this pasture in Brazil was, until recently, lush Amazon rainforest.

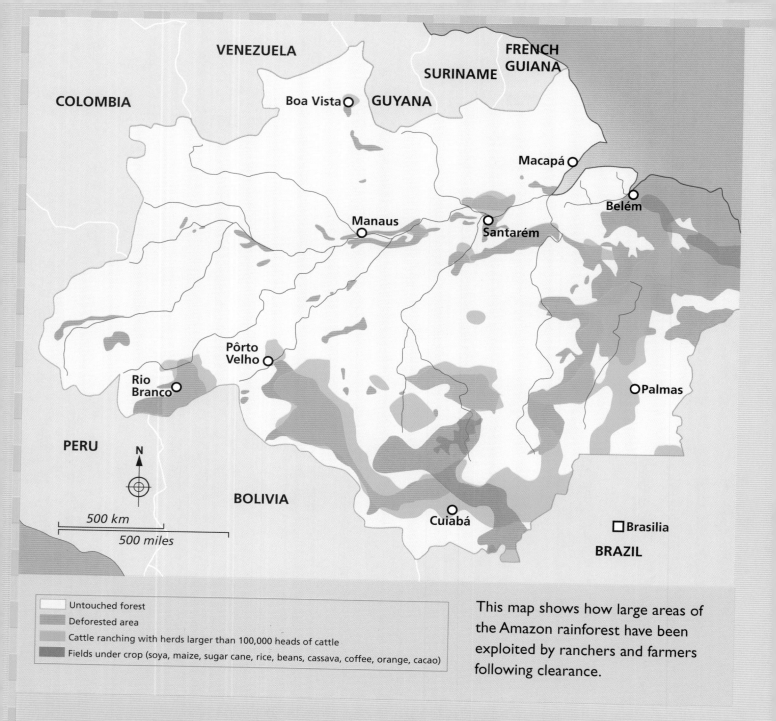

	Untouched forest
	Deforested area
	Cattle ranching with herds larger than 100,000 heads of cattle
	Fields under crop (soya, maize, sugar cane, rice, beans, cassava, coffee, orange, cacao)

This map shows how large areas of the Amazon rainforest have been exploited by ranchers and farmers following clearance.

market and has plans to grow its herds still further. Producing more beef will mean the destruction of more rainforest. Furthermore, the expansion of cattle farming has an impact on the wider environment. Cows emit methane, a greenhouse gas that is an even greater contributor to global warming than carbon dioxide, though it is present in the atmosphere in much smaller quantities.

One way to discourage the expansion of cattle farming would be for governments to impose a 'climate tax' on beef producers.

Another way would be for Western governments to pay cattle ranchers not to destroy any more of the rainforest. As consumers we can help by only eating beef that has been produced locally.

Soya fuels the destruction

After cattle ranching, the biggest cause of rainforest destruction in the Amazon is soya bean plantations. Brazil is currently the world's second biggest exporter of soya beans after the United States. Soya is used as an ingredient in many foods for humans, but, more significantly, it is a major ingredient in animal feed.

Small farmers are clearing areas of forest, not to use themselves but to sell on to large soya-growing companies. Rising demand has increased land values dramatically, further encouraging deforestation. In 1994 a hectare of farmland in the soya-growing state of Mato Grosso, Brazil, was worth about US$100. In 2010, that same land may be worth over US$1,600.

Government action on soya

In 2006 Brazil imposed a moratorium (temporary prohibition) on soya plantations in newly deforested areas. Since then, less than 1 per cent of newly deforested areas have been planted with soya. And in 2008 the Brazilian government committed to reduce deforestation in the Amazon from 11,500 square kilometres the previous year to 9,500 square kilometres.

However, not all farmers observe these restrictions. Around 10 per cent of Brazilian soya is produced on illegal farms that use newly deforested land. They disregard the law that states that 80 per cent of a farm's land should be given over to the rainforest, with only 20 per cent actually being farmed. Nevertheless, the new law has drastically reduced the amount of land being cleared for growing soya beans, and soya is no longer seen as a major threat to the Brazilian Amazon.

CASE STUDY

PROTESTS IN SANTAREM

In 2002 the US company Cargill built two grain silos, a US$20-million terminal and a port in Santarém, in the Brazilian state of Pará. In the two years following this, deforestation around the port increased from 15,000 hectares to 28,000 hectares, land values rocketed and soya production soared as farmers rushed to take advantage of guaranteed sales. Local priest Father Edilberto Sena, an organizer of protests against the plant, said: 'If you fly over Santarém you can see what a desert it has become, you can see the damage of the pesticides and the lonely Brazil nut trees. Cargill has brought devastation to us; this is why we are fighting them.'

3: Roads, Dams and Climate Change

Many of the roads that carve their way through the Amazon rainforest have been built by industries to provide access for mines, logging operations or agribusinesses. Once a paved road has been constructed, lots of unofficial spur roads soon spring up in fishbone patterns, cutting deeper into the forest. These smaller roads open up new areas of previously untouched land to small farmers. They clear this land and grow crops on it for a few years until the soil degrades, then turn it over to cattle grazing and clear yet more forest for crops.

Road to ruin

The BR-163 is a highway that runs 1,760 kilometres north–south from Cuiabá in the soya-growing Mato Grosso, to Santarém in Pará. Much of the route remains unpaved, and it currently costs around US$80 to transport a tonne of soya from the Mato Grosso region to Atlantic ports such as Santarém. However, there are plans to finish the paving of the road. If this were to happen, it would cut the transport cost to just US$50 per tonne, delivering huge savings to the soya-growing agribusinesses in Mato Grosso. It is anticipated that up to 10 million tonnes of soya per year could eventually travel the BR-163, creating annual savings on transport costs of up to US$320 million!

PERSPECTIVES

DANGEROUS DRIVE

Driving along the BR-163 is like taking part in a surreal rural video game. First, you must dodge waves of potholes that home in expertly on your vehicle. Next, ease your way past lumbering grain lorries whose tyres are prone to sudden explosions. As you pass fields of corn and soya, watch out for wandering cattle and the cowboys chasing them. And throughout, beware of kamikaze farm trucks rushing headlong towards you on the wrong side of the road.

Steve Kingstone,
BBC News,
26 September 2006

It is easy to see why this is an attractive idea, not just to the agribusinesses of Mato Grosso, but also to their customers in Europe and China. However, set against this, the environmental costs of road building in the forest are immense. The Belém–Brasilia highway, completed in the

Roads like this one in Brazil could soon be crossing the Amazon. These roads will give access to areas of forest that were previously unreachable.

A truck with a fresh load of soya beans at a soya storage warehouse in Mato Grosso, Brazil. The road-building programme will make Brazil's soya industry ever more profitable.

A new road being built through the Amazon. Roads can have a disastrous effect on rainforest wildlife, disrupting the natural migration of animals.

1970s, has now developed into an area of rainforest destruction 400 kilometres wide! A survey published by the Carnegie Institution in 2008 reported that 75 per cent of rainforest destruction in Peru happened within 19 kilometres of a road, while in Brazil, 95 per cent of deforestation happens within 50 kilometres of a road.

Holding up the roads

Multinational companies are attracted by the savings that could be made by building roads through the rainforest. For example, the Japanese company Honda ships around a million motorcycles to southern Brazil each year at a cost of US$42 per bike. The completion of the BR-163 highway could reduce this cost to US$29 per bike, saving US$12.5 million per year.

If Brazil is to continue its economic development, it needs good road links. This should be possible to achieve without too much cost to the environment, so long as it is not accompanied by the building of unofficial spur roads. If the government could enforce a freeze on unofficial roadbuilding, as well as ban the exploitation of forests surrounding the roads, then Brazil could continue to grow its economy without fatally damaging its forests.

Dams: cleaner, greener energy?

In Brazil, several tributaries of the River Amazon have been used for the creation of hydroelectric power (HEP). This is a means of generating electricity using flowing water. It involves the construction of huge dams across rivers, which lead to the creation of enormous lakes. The water from the lakes is periodically released through the dams via turbines, which spin as the water flows through them. The turbines create electricity as a result of their spinning action.

In one sense HEP is a good form of energy, because it does not produce any carbon dioxide in the creation of electricity. Damming rivers creates huge lakes, but this need not be a problem, and in dry

This area of rainforest was flooded as part of the Tucurui Dam. project. Hydroelectric power generation has had a major impact on the Amazon.

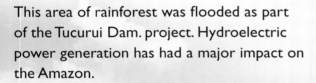

CASE STUDY

TUCURUI DAM

The Tucurui Dam on the Tocantins River in Brazil was completed in 1984. By 2006, an estimated 40 million people were receiving electricity generated by the dam. It produces 8,370 megawatts of electricity per hour, powering three cities. However, its construction flooded 2,430 square kilometres of forest and forced 4,300 families to leave their homes. The dam had a serious impact on fisheries further down the river, causing the loss of many livelihoods. On the positive side, the area around the dam became much more prosperous as new businesses moved in, boosting employment.

parts of the world, it can even be a benefit. However, in species-rich areas such as the Amazon, flooding immense areas of rainforest displaces or destroys many animals and plants. The problem even extends to people – in many cases, tribes have been forced to leave homelands they have lived in for centuries to make way for the new lakes.

The Belo Monte project

In 2010 the Brazilian government approved the construction of a new HEP project in the state of Pará, called Belo Monte. This was a bitter blow for environmentalists, who had campaigned against it for 20 years. Belo Monte will cost around US$17 billion to build. It will involve damming parts of the Xingu River in order to create approximately 11,000 megawatts of electricity per hour – enough to power 23 million homes. However, the project will flood around 500 square kilometres of rainforest. And that might not be the end of the story.

Between June and August, the river flow is weak, and power generation at this time of year is unreliable. To address this issue, the Brazilian government has proposed building another massive dam at Altamira, which would flood a further 6,100 square kilometres of rainforest. No decision has yet been made on this. The Brazilian government has claimed that no native peoples will be displaced by the scheme, despite the fact that the project will flood part of the Xingu Indian reservation.

Alternatives to HEP

In many ways, HEP is the obvious solution to energy production in the Amazon. With populations growing and energy needs increasing, Brazil and its neighbours need to increase their energy production capacity. HEP produces no greenhouse gases and is a clean, renewable energy source. However, HEP requires the flooding of valleys, which destroys hundreds or even thousands of square kilometres of rainforest, threatening the many and diverse species of animals and plants that live there.

PERSPECTIVES

BATTLES OVER BELO MONTE

We want to make sure that Belo Monte does not destroy the ecosystems and the biodiversity that we have taken care of for millennia. We are opposed to dams on the Xingu and will fight to protect our river.

Megaron Tuxucumarrae, Kayapo Indian chief,
February 2010

There is not going to be an environmental disaster. Not a single Indian will be displaced. They will be indirectly affected, but they will not have to leave indigenous lands.

Carlos Minc, Brazilian Environment Minister,
February 2010

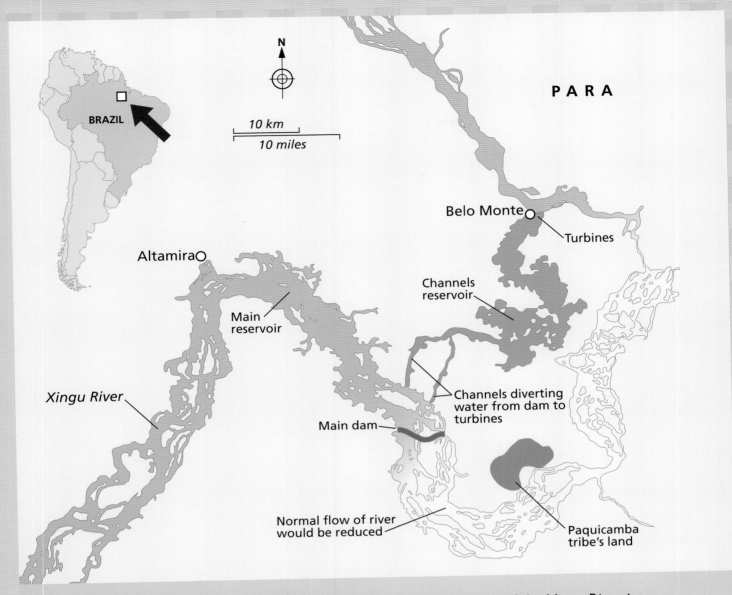

N

BRAZIL

PARA

10 km
10 miles

Belo Monte○
Turbines

Altamira○

Channels
reservoir

Main
reservoir

Channels diverting
water from dam to
turbines

Xingu River

Main dam

Normal flow of river
would be reduced

Paquicamba
tribe's land

The proposed Belo Monte dam project will largely divert the flow of the Xingu River into a newly formed reservoir. This will seriously affect the Paquicamba tribe, living near its present course, who will see the amount of water available to them drastically reduced.

The alternatives all have their own disadvantages. Conventional gas- or coal-fired power stations, though reliable sources of energy, produce huge quantities of carbon dioxide. Nuclear power does not produce any carbon emissions, but spent nuclear fuel remains deadly to humans for thousands of years and has to be stored very carefully. Renewable energy sources like solar panels and wind turbines would involve similar levels of forest destruction to HEP and, at the moment, they are too expensive. In the future, as technology advances and renewable energy generation becomes

Across the world, a hectare of rainforest is lost every second. Tragically, very little will ever recover and regrow.

more affordable, it may be possible for the inhabitants of the forest to produce their own energy through microgeneration; in other words, they may use solar panels and wind turbines to provide the energy they need for themselves. Large-scale solar and wind energy generation is unlikely to be a reality in the Amazon.

The world's problem

Apart from the habitat destruction caused by deforestation, there are other even more worrying reasons why we should be concerned about the clearance of large areas of rainforest. Stored within the world's rainforests are an estimated 610 billion tonnes of carbon. When trees are burned, or even when they are cut down and left to rot, they release the carbon stored within them into the atmosphere, contributing to global carbon dioxide emissions and therefore to climate change. It is scary to think that more carbon dioxide is produced in one day of rainforest destruction than would be caused by more than 8 million people flying from London to New York!

Carbon stores

Destroying the rainforests not only releases carbon dioxide into the atmosphere, it also reduces their capacity to absorb this gas. Rainforests absorb through photosynthesis an estimated 4.8 billion tonnes of carbon dioxide from the atmosphere each year, equivalent to 15 per cent of human carbon dioxide emissions. Rainforest destruction is therefore a major contributor to global warming. Furthermore, when the rainforest disappears, so does the cloud cover, which gives protection from the sun's heat and helps to lower ground temperatures by up to 5°C.

We want to develop, too!

For all these reasons, many people in the developed world believe that, for the sake of the planet, it would be a good idea to encourage rainforested countries not to destroy their forests.

However, rainforested countries argue that the developed countries achieved their economic and industrial power at the expense of their own forests, most of which they cleared centuries ago. Rainforested countries insist that they should also be allowed to develop, and that means converting parts of their rainforest into more productive, wealth-producing land. They should be allowed to clear forested areas for timber or to grow crops or graze cattle.

If developed countries want them to stop doing this, then they must pay them money in compensation. This sounds like common sense, but getting the world's governments to agree on how much to pay will be a huge challenge.

FACTS and FIGURES

CARBON DIOXIDE EMISSIONS

The Intergovernmental Panel on Climate Change (IPCC) estimates that between 7 and 8 billion tonnes of carbon dioxide are released into the atmosphere every year through the destruction of the rainforests. Up to 96 per cent of these emissions are thought to originate from tropical rainforests. The rest come from temperate rainforests. In total, it amounts to about 25 per cent of all human-made carbon dioxide emissions, which is greater than the carbon dioxide produced by either the United States or China in a whole year!

4: Rainforests of South-East Asia

South-East Asia is made up of a 4,960-kilometre-long chain of 20,000 islands, which between them cover 2,880,100 square kilometres. The rainforests of South-East Asia are the oldest on the planet, dating back 70 million years. They are home to even more species of plants and animals than the Amazon or African rainforests. Yet some experts fear that the forests of South-East Asia could be all but destroyed by 2020. This chapter will focus on the issues affecting the rainforests of Indonesia and Papua New Guinea.

Indonesia

Indonesia in South-East Asia is made up of 17,000 islands. It has almost 88.5 million hectares of forested land – 55 per cent of its total land area – and is the world's third largest rainforested zone after the Amazon and the Congo Basin. These forests are now some of the most threatened on the planet. In the space of just 15 years to 2005, 28 million hectares of forest were lost. The causes of the destruction are varied, but most of it is due either to logging or large-scale agriculture.

Indonesia's rainforests are home to 3,305 animal species and at least 29,375 plant species. Over 30 per cent of the animals and almost 60 per cent of the plants are found only in Indonesia. Almost one in ten of its animal species is threatened with extinction as increasing amounts of their forest habitat is destroyed.

Logging in Indonesia

Indonesia is the world's largest exporter of tropical timber, with a trade worth US$5 billlion a year. Logging permits have

FACTS and FIGURES

INDONESIAN EMISSIONS

The burning of the rainforests in Indonesia has made it the world's third largest greenhouse gas emitting country, after the United States and China. Emissions resulting from the destruction of its forests account for an incredible 5 per cent of all human carbon dioxide emissions on the planet!

Source: Rainforest Action Network

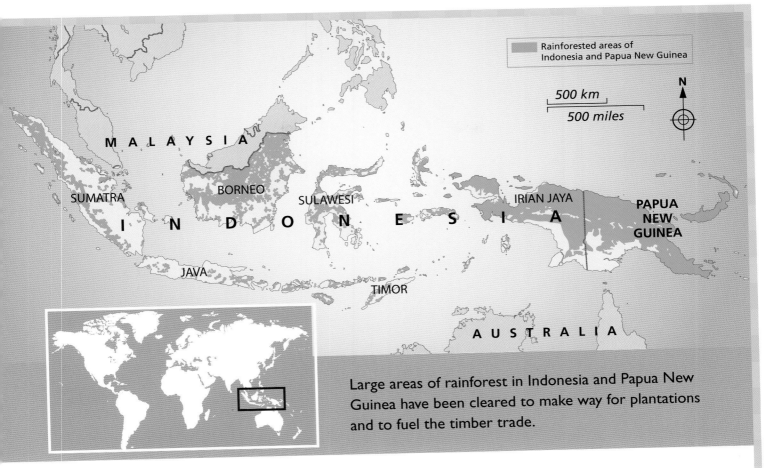

500 km

500 miles

N

MALAYSIA

SUMATRA

BORNEO

SULAWESI

IRIAN JAYA

PAPUA
NEW
GUINEA

INDONESIA

JAVA

TIMOR

AUSTRALIA

Large areas of rainforest in Indonesia and Papua New Guinea have been cleared to make way for plantations and to fuel the timber trade.

been issued for over half of the country's remaining forests (48 million hectares). The timber industry has gradually opened up some of the last great wildernesses on the planet. Areas that were once almost inaccessible are now in reach of the loggers, who are constantly moving deeper into the forests to find suitable trees.

The destruction is happening at an alarming rate. Since the mid-1990s, the number of logging concessions (rights granted by the government) in the remote Irian Jaya region has almost trebled and now makes up 20 per cent of all concessions in Indonesia. Authorized loggers clear between 700,000 and 850,000 hectares of Indonesian rainforest each year. But the Indonesian government claims that up to 75 per cent of logging in Indonesia is illegal. Estimates suggest that up to 2.8 million hectares of rainforest are destroyed annually when illegal logging is taken into account.

Raw logs are regularly smuggled to neighbouring counries, such as Malaysia and Singapore, despite a ban on their export. Underpaid officials are often willing to accept bribes from unscrupulous business people in return for ignoring illegal logging operations.

Papua New Guinea

Papua New Guinea (PNG) shares one of the largest islands in the Indonesian archipelago with the Indonesian state of

LOGGERS IN PAPUA, INDONESIA

More than a quarter of the forests in Papua, Indonesia, have been sold off to logging companies.... [T]hese concessions last between 20 and 30 years. If the Indonesian government does nothing to stop logging concessions, soon all of our forests will be gone.

Christian Poerba,
Executive Director of
Forest Watch Indonesia.

Irian Jaya. Between 1972 and 2002, Papua New Guinea experienced the world's third largest forest losses (after Brazil and Indonesia), with a decline from 38 million hectares to 33 million hectares. A satellite study by the University of Papua New Guinea and the Australian National University, released in 2008, estimated that more than half of its trees could be lost by 2021. Logging and large-scale palm oil plantations are the main causes. When the loggers finish their work, farmers move in to finish clearing the land and then use it for agriculture.

The traditional way of life of forest peoples, like these tribesmen from Papua New Guinea, is under threat. If they die out, their cultures and languages will too.

The forest loss has been very rapid, on a scale similar to that of the Amazon. Current estimates suggest that PNG may lose over half of its remaining rainforest by 2021. This is especially disturbing because Papua New Guinea's rainforests contain over 6 per cent of the world's land species. They are also home to a surprising human cultural diversity, with 830 languages spoken there – more than 10 per cent of all languages spoken on Earth! Many of these are the languages of the tribes living in the country's rainforests. If their way of life is lost, the chances are that their languages will die out also.

Papua New Guinea has been struggling with a rapidly increasing population and has one of the highest rates of population growth in the world. With over 6 million mouths to feed, more and more forested land is being cleared to make way for crops. This is understandable, but if the rest of the world wishes to save Papua New Guinea's rainforests, they will have to find another way of feeding the country's people.

Palm oil in Indonesia

Since 2002, land has increasingly been cleared to make way for oil-palm plantations.

Palm oil is a very cheap vegetable oil found in many of the products we consume. It is also used to create biodiesel, a fuel made from plants. Bearing in mind that oil supplies could be used up within the next

20 to 30 years, *growing* our fuel seems like a good solution to the coming energy crisis.

Between 2005 and 2010, demand for palm oil trebled in the United States. It is also set to become increasingly important in Europe. The European Union's Directive on the Promotion of the Use of Biofuels and Other Renewable Fuels for Transport (2003) states that by 31 December 2010, 5.75 per cent of all fuel currently sold in Europe must be biofuel, and this must increase to 13 per cent by 2020. Most diesel now contains about 5 per cent palm oil.

Yet biofuels come with a substantial cost to the environment. To make space for palm oil plantations, large areas of rainforest are slashed and burned. This releases huge amounts of carbon dioxide into the atmosphere. It has been estimated that it would take a palm oil plantation up to 840 years to soak up the carbon released by burning the forest to make way for it!

Yet each year in Indonesia, hundreds of thousands of hectares of forest are set alight before the monsoon season to make space for palm oil plantations. If the monsoon rains are delayed, fires can burn unchecked. This happened in Indonesia in 1997–98 when over 2 million hectares of forest were destroyed. Satellite analysis of the fires showed that 80 per cent were linked to plantations or logging concessions. Burning is the fastest way to clear land for new plantations, but logged areas are also more likely to burn than untouched rainforest. This is because, after logging, debris is left on the ground, which can fuel fires. Also, without the shading effect of the canopy, the forest floor dries out, making fires more likely.

CASE STUDY

KALIMANTAN

In the Indonesian territory of Kalimantan on the island of Borneo, a 2-million-hectare oil-palm plantation is planned. This has caused real concern to environmentalists, as there are still potentially so many unknown plant and animal species in Borneo – 361 new species were discovered there between 1994 and 2004.

Palm oil in Papua New Guinea

Palm oil plantations are also springing up at an alarming rate in PNG. Vast areas of virgin forest are being swept aside to make way for the endless rows of palm trees. The local people are banding together to try and stop the plantations. They have seen what has happened elsewhere and are determined to protect PNG's forests. However, the multinational companies responsible for the rainforest clearances have huge economic power, which they use to get their way. In PNG, 97 per cent of the land is community-owned, so to establish their plantations, big

A plantation worker harvests palm fruits in Indonesia's South Sulawesi province. Indonesia was the world's top producer of palm oil in 2009, producing 20.9 million tonnes.

companies obtain long-term leases that strip people of control. One of the methods companies use is to set up 'mini-estates' in which communities enter into partnerships with companies. The companies charge them for setting up new plantations and take 90 per cent of the profits. The people have to continue to plant oil palms on their estate until their debts are paid off.

Solutions for South-East Asia

'People power' is having some effect in PNG, but it will take more than that to ensure a safe future for its forests. In Indonesia, meanwhile, the situation is even more troubled. So long as officials are prepared to turn a blind eye to large-scale illegal logging, it is hard to see how its rainforests can be protected.

Is REDD the answer?

One possible solution to the problem would be for the rest of the world to pay rainforested countries not to exploit their forests. This idea was proposed by PNG and nine other rainforest nations in 2005. They called it 'reducing emissions from deforestation and forest degradation', or REDD. They argue that, as the whole world benefits from the rainforests' survival, the whole world should pay towards their protection. Under a REDD scheme, rainforested countries would be compensated by the rest of the world for protecting their rainforests, rather than clearing them.

It is estimated that in 2007, up to 73 million tonnes of carbon dioxide were released through the burning of PNG's rainforests. If the world placed a nominal value of US$5 on each tonne of carbon dioxide saved, this would amount to US$365 million for the year. This far exceeds the official figure for the amount earned – US$189 million – from timber exports from PNG for that year, and would therefore act as a tremendous incentive for the PNG government to protect its rainforests.

The idea appears to make a lot of sense. However, the countries of the world will struggle to agree on how to value a tonne of carbon dioxide. International climate change conferences, such as those in Bali in 2007 and Copenhagen in 2009, have so far failed to reach agreement on this issue. Meanwhile, the forests continue to burn.

PERSPECTIVES

A PAPER AGREEMENT

This isn't anything more than a paper agreement if the financing isn't there to back it up.

Becky Chacko, Director of Climate Policy, Conservation International. speaking about REDD at the 2009 Copenhagen Climate Change Conference

Sustainable biofuel certification

In June 2010 the European Union proposed a new voluntary code to certify biofuels for sustainability, ensuring that they are not sourced from oil-palm plantations that have been created by destroying rainforest. This is a step in the right direction, but the code needs to be international, or else palm oil traders will simply sell their wares to other parts of the world with less stringent controls.

Nature reserves

Another way of protecting the rainforests is to set up nature reserves. In September 2004 the Indonesian government responded to pressure from European and Japanese environmental groups by creating an 'ecosystem restoration concession', a 101,000-hectare nature reserve of lowland rainforest in Sumatra, Indonesia. The reserve, known as the Harapan Forest, is home to 267 bird species, 66 of which are at risk of extinction, as well as endangered mammals such as the Sumatran tiger, Asian elephant and clouded leopard.

Orang-utans are endangered in Borneo because of habitat destruction. There are thought to be no more than 69,000 of them left.

5: Rainforests of the Congo Basin

The Congo Basin in Africa is the world's second largest area of rainforest. It covers parts of Cameroon, the Central African Republic, the Democratic Republic of Congo (DRC), the Republic of Congo, Equatorial Guinea and Gabon. More than 75 million people depend on the forests for their existence. The forests are also home to some of Africa's best known wild animals, including chimpanzees, gorillas and forest elephants.

Taxation and corruption

In recent years, the forests of the Congo Basin have been badly damaged by commercial logging and destruction for subsistence agriculture (small-scale agriculture by farmers for themselves and their families only), both of which have been caused, indirectly at least, by civil war. Logging has increased significantly since peace returned to the region as countries desperately try to generate new wealth.

The governments in the Congo Basin impose taxes on the logging companies. Officially, the revenue raised from these taxes is to pay for the provision of health care, education and other essential services for the poor people of the region. Instead, it mainly ends up in the pockets of corrupt officials. In many areas, enforcement officers, who are supposed to prevent illegal logging operations, are ill-equipped to do their job. Often they have only bicycles to patrol huge areas of rainforest!

The indigenous people of the forests are offered pathetic 'gifts' by the logging companies, such as bags of salt or crates of beer, in return for the destruction of the places where they live. The logging companies have promised them hospitals, schools and proper sanitation, but they are often are left with nothing and are simply

FACTS and FIGURES

LOGGING IN THE DRC

There has been a moratorium on logging in place since 2002, but despite this, over 15 million hectares of the DRC's forest have been sold to the logging industry. That's an area five times larger than Belgium!

Greenpeace

forced to move to new areas as the forest they depend on for food and shelter is destroyed around them.

Roads open up the forests

A network of roads is expanding rapidly through the Congo Basin rainforest. Researchers have studied satellite photographs of 10.4 million square kilometres of Congo Basin rainforest, taken between 1976 and 2003, and found 52,000 kilometres of logging roads.

Just as elsewhere in rainforested areas, the roads provide access to areas of forest that were previously difficult or impossible to reach. Once the loggers have moved on, the small farmers can move into an area, burn off the remaining forest and plant crops.

During the 1990s and early 2000s, civil war in the DRC drove many people from their homes. The roads gave these refugees access to new land, enabling them to clear forest and grow food.

Pygmy tribes

The Congo is the world's second largest river by volume after the Amazon, and its rainforests comprise about 70 per cent of Africa's plant cover. The forests teem with

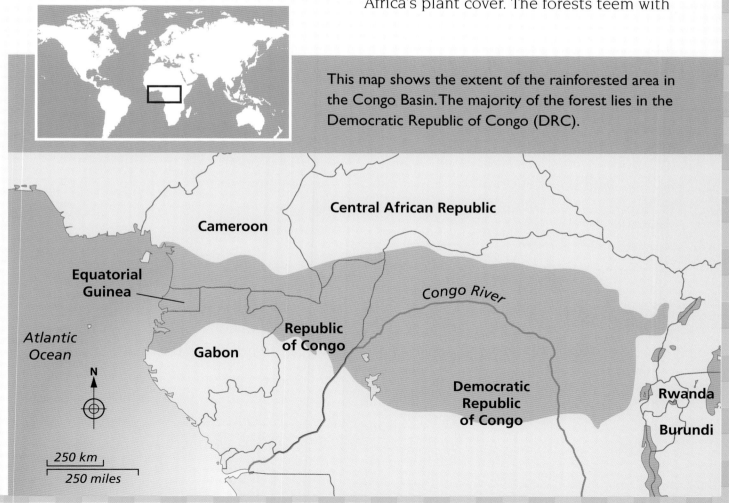

This map shows the extent of the rainforested area in the Congo Basin. The majority of the forest lies in the Democratic Republic of Congo (DRC).

Central African Republic

Cameroon

Equatorial Guinea

Congo River

Atlantic Ocean

Republic of Congo

Gabon

N

Democratic Republic of Congo

Rwanda

Burundi

250 km
250 miles

life, with over 600 tree species and 10,000 animal species. They are also inhabited by Pygmy tribes, including the Mbuti of northern DRC, the Twa of eastern DRC, Rwanda and Burundi, the Baka of southern Cameroon and the Aka of the Central African Republic and northern Congo. In total there are about 150,000 of these forest peoples spread over a huge area, averaging less than one person for every four square kilometres.

Pygmies are small in stature. Even the tallest of the tribes, the Mbuti, rarely grow taller than 1.5 metres. Being small has obviously proved an advantage in the dense forests, as it makes moving about through the trees much easier. Smaller body area also allows Pygmies to dissipate body heat better – a big advantage in the hot and steamy conditions of the rainforest.

The Pygmies live in small groups of up to 70 people, and move several times a year to different parts of the forest to find fresh food supplies, carrying all that they own on their backs. Their nomadic way of life has very little impact on the rainforest, because they never over-exploit any one area.

When tribes set up a new settlement, they clear away the undergrowth and small trees but they leave the canopy, giving shelter from the sun and the rain. They live in houses that look like igloos, but which are made from saplings and leaves woven together to form a shelter.

Pygmy poachers

Pygmies are excellent hunters, but traditionally never took more game than they needed and had a great respect for their prey. Now, these forest peoples are increasingly being hired as trackers by poachers (illegal hunters of protected animals) who are trying to find forest elephants. Pygmies are also hunting for more and more 'bushmeat' (the meat of wild African animals) to trade with the villagers who fled to the rainforests during the recent civil wars.

CASE STUDY

LOGGERS AND PYGMIES

Logging is a massive threat to the Pygmies' way of life, as it destroys the forests the Pygmies need to survive. Logging roads open up the forests, bringing lots of new settlers from other areas, some of whom will carry diseases that the Pygmies have no immunity to because they have never encountered them before. The loggers bring new items to trade, including tobacco, marijuana and alcohol – substances that many Pygmies have grown addicted to. Loggers also bring a whole new idea with them – money – and this encourages the Pygmies to exploit their forests in a way they never have before. There is a real danger that without protection, the forest people's way of life will be lost forever.

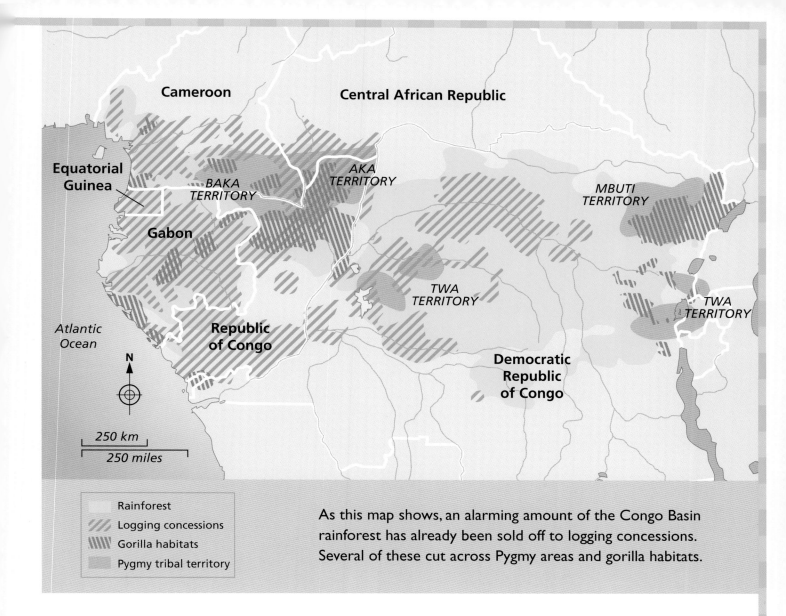

Rainforest
Logging concessions
Gorilla habitats
Pygmy tribal territory

As this map shows, an alarming amount of the Congo Basin rainforest has already been sold off to logging concessions. Several of these cut across Pygmy areas and gorilla habitats.

Refugees in the rainforest

The civil war in the DRC has forced huge numbers of its people to relocate. Around 375,000 of them are thought to have taken shelter within the boundaries of the country's Virunga National Park, home to more than half of the world's remaining population of mountain gorillas.

All of these people need wood to burn on their cooking fires, to build their houses and to make tools. The park's area of pristine rainforest is shrinking because of all the trees these newcomers are chopping down. Aid agencies and the United Nations supply these people with sufficient wood to meet their needs, so they do not have to cut down more of the forest, but this cannot be a long-term solution. Instead, the settlers are being trained to look after the protected areas and are being shown how preserving their forests for the future can encourage tourism in the region. Tourists, who come

These refugees of the civil war in the DRC have been forced to seek refuge in the rainforest after their homes were attacked by soldiers.

from much wealthier countries in the West, spend lots of money while they are on holiday and much of this money will find its way to the local people.

The bushmeat trade

With so many very poor people living in the rainforest, it's not surprising that some turn to poaching to feed themselves. Unfortunately, they are targeting endangered mountain gorillas and forest

CASE STUDY

MASTER MAPPERS

People in the Congo Basin rarely own the land they live on, even if they have been there for many years, so there is nothing to stop governments from selling it to loggers. The charity, Rainforest Foundation UK, has trained Congolese 'Master Mappers' to travel into the remote Inongo territory in western DRC, where they are working with nearly 100 rainforest villages. The Master Mappers are teaching 660 villagers to use GPS devices (instruments that use satellite signals to determine location) to produce detailed maps that will prove their existence to loggers and to the DRC government. This will hopefully prevent more logging concessions in the area.

elephants. If this situation continues, some of these spectacular large mammals could face extinction. A similar story is unfolding across the Congo Basin, with elephants being hunted in the forests of Cameroon for their ivory tusks. They are also being killed to prevent them from damaging farms: if a herd of elephants raids a smallholding, a farmer's entire annual harvest can be ruined.

Solutions

Conservation charities and aid agencies are working with forest communities to show them how valuable their forests could be as tourist areas. They are also training people to help preserve protected areas. In many areas, the government has imposed bans on bushmeat trading. In Cameroon, villagers are being trained to use trenches and fencing around their smallholdings to stop elephants from ruining their crops.

Increasingly, the elephants are being monitored by agencies like the World

Gorillas reproduce quite slowly, at about the quarter of the rate of most mammals. The targeting of gorillas by hunters has had a disastrous effect on their numbers.

Wildlife Fund, using electronic tags. This helps to detect incidents of poaching and also enables researchers to learn more about elephant behaviour. WWF and other environmental groups use their global influence to try to ban trade in ivory. If successful, this will remove any incentive for poaching.

Mining

The Congo Basin is rich in mineral deposits, including iron, copper, manganese, uranium, gold and diamonds. This fact has not escaped the attention of international mining companies, some of which have managed to secure very lucrative deals. New mining operations cause deforestation and water pollution. Also, the roads and railways that provide the means to get the minerals from mine to market open up previously inaccessible areas of forest for bushmeat hunting and poaching.

The Belinga Project

In July 2007 the government of Gabon agreed a deal with CMEC, a Chinese mining company, to create an iron ore mine in the Gabonese rainforest. The Belinga Project, as it was known, would cover some 7,700 square kilometres of land and, as well as the mine, would also include the construction of a hydroelectric dam near Kongou Falls. The mining road would be carved straight through Ivindo National Park, a 3,000-square-kilometre conservation area that is home to chimpanzees, western lowland gorillas, buffalo and forest elephants.

The Gabonese government failed to carry out a proper assessment of the environmental impact of this project. Nor did it consult properly with the local people about how the project would affect them. The mine, once built, would destroy entire ecosystems, while the damming of the Ivindo River would flood villages and drive numerous animal species from their homes. By giving the go-ahead for the project, the government broke its own code on national parks. The code states that the national parks were established to preserve 'the wealth of the ecosystem … for current and future generations' and to encourage 'the development of ecotourism as an economic alternative to the exploitation of natural resources'.

A group called Brainforest, led by prize-winning environmentalist Marc Ona Essangui, helped the affected communities to organize protests against the mine and dam project. The Gabonese government met with the protesters and agreed to look at the project again. In May 2008 the deal was renegotiated on terms that were more sensitive to environmental concerns. The project was scaled down to just 600 square kilometres and there would be no road building through the national park.

PERSPECTIVES

FLOODED LAND, POLLUTED WATERS

All the villages upstream of the dam will be flooded and people displaced. People drink the water of the river and fish in it; they'll lose their livelihoods. Near the mine, the water will be polluted.

Gabonese environmental activist
Marc Ona Essangui

Mines like this gold mine in the DRC bring people deep into the rainforest in search of their fortunes. Deforestation and pollution tend to be the results of such operations, many of which are poorly regulated.

6: The Future of the Forests

The world's rainforests are home to millions of people and vast numbers of animal and plant species. Almost certainly there remain thousands of species still waiting to be discovered, many of which may hold cures to the diseases that ail us. Furthermore, the rainforests play a crucial role in maintaining the Earth's climate and acting as a check against global warming. We destroy them at our peril.

A global challenge

Humans are waking up to the fact that rainforests make a massive contribution to the world's climate, and we destroy them at our peril. Billions of tonnes of carbon dioxide are locked away in the forests. By destroying the forests, we release more greenhouse gases into the atmosphere. This is the most likely reason why the planet's rainforests will be preserved. The developed world is coming round to the view that rainforests have much more value to the planet as they are than they do as timber, paper, beans or oil.

In this book, we have tried to show why it is essential that we protect these amazing environments for the future, not just to save the people, animals and plants that live there, but also to ensure that we prevent climate change from spiralling out of control. We can only hope that humanity will agree in time to value the rainforests as they are.

Can you help?

The problems facing the rainforests are so massive, you'd be forgiven for wondering what kind of a difference one person could make. Well, it's true that your influence as an individual may be small, but if enough individuals act together, they can make a difference. Action could include supporting organizations that campaign for rainforests, as well as influencing those around you, like your family, in what they do and buy.

Use consumer power

Next time you're shopping, look out for either a 'Fair Trade' logo or a 'Rainforest Alliance' logo on the foods you buy. These labels show that the farmers who grew the crop received a fair payment for it and that their labourers enjoyed good working and living conditions. They show that the crop was grown on a farm committed to protecting the environment.

SAVE THE FORESTS

If we do nothing else, save the rain forest ... most biologists believe that the rapid destruction of the tropical rain forests and the irretrievable loss of the living species dying along with them, represent the single most serious damage to nature now occurring.

Earth in the Balance: Forging a New Common Purpose by Al Gore (Earthscan Publications, 2007)

A cause for hope: in this part of the Amazon rainforest, palm tree seedlings have been planted to help the forest regenerate itself.

Avoid palm oil

Look at the ingredients of the products in the supermarket. If an item contains palm oil and it doesn't say it has been sustainably grown, avoid it! Rainforest will have been destroyed to make way for the palms.

Ethical wood

When buying products made from tropical wood, like furniture or paper, look out for the FSC (Forest Stewardship Council) mark, which shows that the wood has come from managed forests.

Adopt your own rainforest

There are schemes that allow you to adopt an acre (0.4 hectare) of rainforest in return for a donation. Your money is used to buy new land, to plant trees and to pay staff to look after the forest and prevent poaching. Please note, you don't actually get to own the forest you adopt.

Glossary

agribusiness A large-scale farming enterprise.

biodiversity The range and variety of species to be found within a given habitat.

biofuel A fuel produced from dry organic matter or combustible oils produced by plants.

canopy The top layer of trees, which act like a roof for the rainforest.

climate change Long-term, significant change in the Earth's climate, usually seen as resulting from human activity.

conservation Preservation of the natural environment.

deforestation The clearing and destruction of forested areas.

developed countries The wealthiest nations in the world, including Western Europe, the United States, Canada, Japan, Australia and New Zealand.

ecosystem A community of living things plus the physical environment they depend on.

endangered species A species whose numbers are so small that the species is at risk of extinction.

erode (Of rocks and other deposits on the Earth's surface) Be gradually worn away by the action of water, ice, wind and other natural agents.

European Union (EU) An economic and political association of European countries.

exploitation Taking advantage of.

global warming An increase in the temperature of the Earth. Global warming has occurred in the distant past as the result of the Earth's natural cycles, but today the term is used to refer to the warming linked to human activity.

greenhouse gases Gases that trap the Sun's heat in the atmosphere.

habitat The environment in which an animal or plant normally lives or grows.

hydroelectric power (HEP) Electric power generated by using flowing water to drive a turbine that powers a generator.

humidity The amount of water vapour in the atmosphere.

indigenous Originating in and characteristic of a particular region or country.

multinational company A business that operates in more than one country.

nature reserve An area of land that is managed in order to preserve its wildlife, vegetation and physical features.

nutrients Substances that provide essential nourishment for plants and animals.

photosynthesis The process by which plants convert sunlight, water and carbon dioxide into food, oxygen and water. They 'breathe in' carbon dioxide and 'breathe out' oxygen.

plantation A large estate on which crops are raised, often by resident workers.

sequester Lock away.

shifting cultivation A farming system in which farmers move on from one place to another when the land becomes exhausted.

subsistence farming A type of farming where all the produce is consumed by the farming family.

sustainable Conserving the environment by avoiding depletion of natural resources.

temperate Characterized by moderate temperatures.

Further Information

Books

Essential Habitats: Tropical Rainforest Habitats by Barbara Taylor (TickTock Books, 2009)

Global Questions: Why Are The Rainforests Being Destroyed? by Peter Littlewood (Franklin Watts Ltd, 2010)

Horrible Geography: Bloomin' Rainforests by Anita Ganeri (Scholastic, 2008)

Planet Earth: Rainforests by Steve Parker (QED Publishing, 2009)

Protecting Habitats: Rainforests in Danger by Moira Butterfield (Franklin Watts Ltd, 2008)

Websites

www.greenpeace.org
Website for the campaigning organization, with lots of news on rainforests.

www.rainforest-alliance.org
A very good site, with comprehensive information on the Rainforest Alliance's work.

www.rainforestconcern.org
A great site from this UK-based rainforest charity. It contains information on their work, and excellent resources for education.

www.rainforestfoundationuk.org
Website for the Rainforest Foundation, with plenty of information on their work in Central and South America, and good resources for young people too.

www.savetherainforest.org
This website contains some good information about rainforest plants and animals and the threats they face.

Index

Page numbers in **bold** refer to maps and photos.